TJH

D0358651

**Candletown**

Can you find Puddle Lane?

*USING THIS BOOK*

*Children learn to read by **reading**, but they need help to begin with.*

*When you have read the story on the left-hand pages aloud to the child, go back to the beginning of the book and look at the pictures together.*

*Encourage children to read the sentences under the pictures. If they don't know a word, give them a chance to 'guess' what it is from the illustrations, before telling them.*

There are more suggestions for helping children to learn to read in the *Parent/Teacher* booklet.

British Library Cataloguing in Publication Data

McCullagh, Sheila K.
   The wideawake mice go to market. —
(Puddle Lane. Stage 2. 8)
   1. Readers — 1950-
   I. Title      II. Theobalds, Prue      III. Series
   428.6      PE1119

   ISBN 0-7214-0933-4

First edition

Published by Ladybird Books Ltd  Loughborough  Leicestershire  UK
Ladybird Books Inc  Lewiston  Maine 04240  USA

Printed in England

# The Wideawake Mice go to market

*written by* SHEILA McCULLAGH
*illustrated by* PRUE THEOBALDS

This book belongs to:

_____

Ladybird Books

One day, Gita went out
into Puddle Lane.
The sun was shining
and it was very hot.
Gita tied a red handkerchief
over her head, and ran up the lane
to the Magician's house.

Gita ran up Puddle Lane
to the Magician's house.

As Gita got to the gate
that led into the garden,
she saw a little mouse
sitting on the wall in the sunshine.
The little mouse was wearing
a long skirt, a blouse, and a hat.
(Gita didn't know it, but
the little mouse was Aunt Jane.)
At that moment, a puff of wind
blew Gita's handkerchief off.
But Gita was so surprised
to see the little mouse
that she didn't notice.
Aunt Jane saw her, and
disappeared over the wall.
Gita ran back down the lane
to tell Hari.

Gita saw a little mouse
on the wall.

But before she found Hari,
Gita met Mrs Pitter-Patter.
"Oh, Mrs Pitter-Patter," cried Gita.
"There's a mouse on the garden wall.
And the mouse is wearing
a skirt and a hat!"

"Don't tell such stories, Gita,"
said Mrs Pitter-Patter.
"Mice don't wear hats."

"This one does," said Gita.

"Gita, you mustn't tell stories!"
said Mrs Pitter-Patter.
She shook her finger at Gita,
and went off up the lane.
Gita went to find Hari.

# Gita and Mrs Pitter-Patter

9

Aunt Jane ran back
to the big hole
under the hollow tree.
On her way, she saw
Gita's red handkerchief,
which the wind had blown
into the garden.
She went down into the hole,
and found the other mice
all talking together.

Aunt Jane ran back
to the big hole
under the tree.

Uncle Maximus was talking
louder than any of the others.
"I'm hungry," said Uncle Maximus.
"I'm **very** hungry."

"We're **all** hungry,"
said Grandfather Mouse.

"It's market day tomorrow,"
said Chestnut. "I always go
to the market on market day.
You can find food there."

"Then we'll all go to the market,"
said Grandfather Mouse.

"I'm hungry,"
said Uncle Maximus.
"I'm **very** hungry."

"We will all go
to the market,"
said Grandfather Mouse.

"We can't **all** go to market,"
said Chestnut.
"Tom Cat will be there.
Tom Cat is hungry too, you know.
If we all go to market,
Tom Cat would be sure
to catch one of us."
That made everyone shiver.
"I — I'm not very well,"
said Uncle Maximus.
"I think I'll stay at home.
You can bring something back
for me to eat."

"We can't all go to market,"
said Chestnut.
"Tom Cat will be there."

"I'll go to market tomorrow,"
said Chestnut.
"Jeremy and Miranda
can come with me.
They can run the fastest.
The rest of you had better
stay at home.
We'll bring food back with us."
Grandfather Mouse wanted to go too,
but Chestnut said
that he was much too slow,
and Grandmother Mouse said that
he had a cold.

"I will go to market,"
said Chestnut.
"Jeremy and Miranda
can come with me."

Aunt Jane said nothing.
She went back to the garden.
She found Gita's handkerchief,
and pulled it into the hole.
Then she cut it up, and made
four little red sacks.
"What are they for?" asked Chestnut.

"To take to market," said Aunt Jane.

"But there are four of them,"
said Chestnut.
"I'm going to market, too,"
said Aunt Jane.
And she said it so firmly,
that Chestnut didn't say any more.

Aunt Jane made four sacks.
''I'm going to market, too,''
she said.

The next morning, before it was light,
the four little mice
went down Puddle Lane.
Each little mouse
had a little red sack.
They were all going to market.

The four little mice
went down Puddle Lane.
They were all going to market.

As they came to the end
of Puddle Lane,
they saw the big dog.
He was fast asleep.
"Sh!" whispered Chestnut.
"Don't wake him."
They tip-toed past.
The dog's nose twitched.
He dreamt about mice,
but he didn't wake up.

They saw the big dog.
He was fast asleep.

It was just getting light
when they came to the market building.
The four little mice
ran up a post.
They hid in the roof,
and waited.

The four little mice
ran up a post.
They hid in the roof.

They hadn't long to wait.
Soon, they heard people
in the market below.
The four little mice looked down.
The people were setting up tables.
There were bowls of nuts,
and big round cheeses.
There were cakes and biscuits
and loaves of bread.
"I'm hungry," said Jeremy.
"I'm **very** hungry."

The four little mice
looked down.
They saw nuts and cheeses.
Jeremy said, ''I'm hungry.
I'm very hungry.''

"Wait until the market
is full of people," said Chestnut.
"Then they won't see us.
They'll be too busy shopping."
As soon as the people
came into the market,
the little mice ran down the post.
Nobody noticed them.
They ran about the floor,
looking for food.

The little mice
ran down the post.

They began to eat.
They ate cheese and nuts.
They ate cake and biscuits.
(People were very careless,
and dropped all kinds of things
on the floor.)
When they couldn't eat any more,
the four little mice
filled the red sacks with food.
The sacks were soon full.

They ate cheese and nuts.
They filled the sacks.
The sacks were soon full.

"We'll go home now,"
said Aunt Jane.
At that moment, Chestnut
saw Mrs Pitter-Patter.
Mrs Pitter-Patter had come to market,
and her shopping basket was full.
She put down her basket,
while she took out her purse
to pay for a cheese.

Chestnut saw
Mrs Pitter-Patter.
Mrs Pitter-Patter
put down her basket.

"Quick!" said Chestnut.
"Hide in the basket.
We'll get a ride home.
That will be **much** safer
than running across the square."
As quickly as they could, all the mice
picked up their sacks, and hid
in Mrs Pitter-Patter's basket.
Mrs Pitter-Patter put away her purse.
She picked up her basket,
and set off for Puddle Lane.

The mice hid in
Mrs Pitter-Patter's basket.

Mrs Pitter-Patter came to her house
in Puddle Lane.
She put down the basket,
and took out her key.
"Now we must run," said Chestnut.

"Wait until I see if it's safe,"
said Aunt Jane.
And she ran out on to
the handle of the basket.

Mrs Pitter-Patter
put down the basket.
Aunt Jane ran out.

Mrs Pitter-Patter bent down
to pick up her basket.
She saw Aunt Jane
sitting on the handle.
"Help!" cried Mrs Pitter-Patter.
"Help! Help!"
She ran into the house.
She left the basket in Puddle Lane.
Miranda and Jeremy,
Aunt Jane and Chestnut,
all scrambled out,
and ran off up the lane.

Mrs Pitter-Patter saw
Aunt Jane.
She ran into the house.
She left the basket
in Puddle Lane.

There was a great feast that night
in the hole under the tree.
Aunt Jane and Chestnut,
Miranda and Jeremy
were so full, that they couldn't
eat very much.
But they all had a wonderful time.

As for Mrs Pitter-Patter,
she never again told Gita
that she was telling stories.

# Notes for the parent/teacher

When you have read the story, go back to the beginning. Look at each picture and talk about it, pointing to the caption below, and reading it aloud yourself.

Run your finger along under the words as you read, so that the child learns that reading goes from left to right. (You needn't say this in so many words. Children learn many useful things about reading by just reading with you, and it is often better to let them learn by experience, rather than by explanation.) When you next go through the book, encourage the child to read the words and sentences under the illustrations.

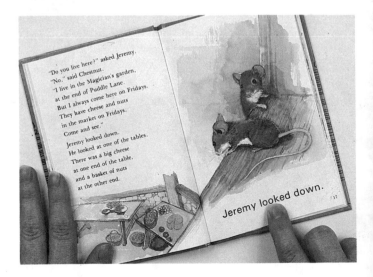

Jeremy looked down.

*Don't rush in with the word before she\* has time to think, but don't leave her struggling for too long. Always encourage her to feel that she is reading successfully, praising her when she does well, and avoiding criticism.*

*Now turn back to the beginning, and print the child's name in the space on the title page, using ordinary, not capital letters. Let her watch you print it: this is another useful experience.*

*Children enjoy hearing the same story many times. Read this one as often as the child likes hearing it. The more opportunities she has of looking at the illustrations and **reading** the captions with you, the more she will come to recognise the words. Don't worry if she **remembers** rather than **reads** the captions. This is a normal stage in learning.*

*If you have a number of books, let her choose which story she would like to have again.*

---

\**Footnote:* In order to avoid the continual "he or she", "him or her", the child is referred to in this book as "she". However, the stories are equally appropriate to boys and girls.

*Have you read these books about the*
*Wideawake Mice?*

### Stage 1

*Hickory Mouse*

### Stage 3

*from The Wideawake Mice*